A Home
for Me

Houseboat

Lola M. Schaefer

Heinemann Library
Chicago, Illinois

©2003 Reed Educational & Professional Publishing
Published by Heinemann Library,
an imprint of Reed Educational & Professional Publishing
Chicago, IL

Customer Service 888-454-2279
Visit our website at www.heinemannlibrary.com

Designed by Sue Emerson, Heinemann Library
Printed and bound in the United States by Lake Book Manufacturing, Inc.

07 06 05 04 03
10 9 8 7 6 5 4 3 2 1

Library of Congress Cataloging-in-Publication Data
Lola M. Schaefer
    Houseboat / Lola M. Schaefer.
       p. cm. — (A Home for Me)
Includes index.
Contents: What is a houseboat?—What do houseboats look like?—How big are houseboats?—How many rooms are in a houseboat?—Where do people talk or play in a houseboat?—Where do people cook in a houseboat?—Where do people sleep in a houseboat?—Where do people bathe in a houseboat?—Where do people clean clothes in a houseboat?—Houseboat map quiz—Houseboat picture glossary.
    ISBN: 1-4034-0262-0 (HC), 1-4034-0485-2 (Pbk.)
    1. Houseboats—Juvenile literature. 2. Boat living—Juvenile literature. [1. Houseboats. 2. Boat living.] I. Title.
II. Series: Schaefer, Lola M., 1950–. Home for me.
    GV836.S33 2002
    797.1'29—dc21
                                       2001008145

Acknowledgments
The author and publishers are grateful to the following for permission to reproduce copyright material:
p. 4 Gibson/Houseboat Magazine; pp. 5, 6, 7, 8T, 12, 13, 14, 20 Courtesy of Houseboat Magazine; pp. 8B, 9, 19 Kort Duce/Houseboat Magazine; pp. 15, 16, 17, 18, 21 Greg Williams/Heinemann Library; p. 23 (row 1, L-R) Courtesy of Houseboat Magazine, Greg Williams/Heinemann Library, Heinemann Library; p. 23 (row 2, L-R) Greg Williams/ Heinemann Library, Jeff Greenberg/Visuals Unlimited, Greg Williams/Heinemann Library; p. 23 (row 3) Courtesy of Houseboat Magazine; back cover (L-R) Greg Williams/Heinemann Library, Courtesy of Houseboat Magazine

Cover photograph courtesy of Houseboat Magazine
Photo research by Amor Montes de Oca
Special thanks to our models, the Jackson family, and to Starved Rock Adventures for the use of their location.

Every effort has been made to contact copyright holders of any material reproduced in this book. Any omissions will be rectified in subsequent printings if notice is given to the publisher.

Special thanks to our advisory panel for their help in the preparation of this book:

Eileen Day, Preschool teacher
Chicago, IL

Ellen Dolmetsch,
Library Media Specialist
Wilmington, DE

Kathleen Gilbert,
Second Grade Teacher
Round Rock, TX

Sandra Gilbert,
Library Media Specialist
Houston, TX

Angela Leeper,
Educational Consultant
North Carolina Department
of Public Instruction
Raleigh, NC

Pam McDonald,
Reading Support Specialist
Winter Springs, FL

Melinda Murphy,
Library Media Specialist
Houston, TX

Some words are shown in bold, **like this.**
You can find them in the picture glossary on page 23.

Contents

What Is a Houseboat?

A houseboat is a house that floats on water.

Motors move houseboats from one place to another.

motor

Some people live on a houseboat all the time.

Other people stay on a houseboat just for a short time.

What Do Houseboats Look Like?

Most houseboats look like **rectangles**.

Most houseboats are light colors.

decks

Houseboats have **decks**.

They have large doors and many windows.

How Big Are Houseboats?

Houseboats can be small or large.

Houseboats are about as long as four cars.

How Many Rooms Are in a Houseboat?

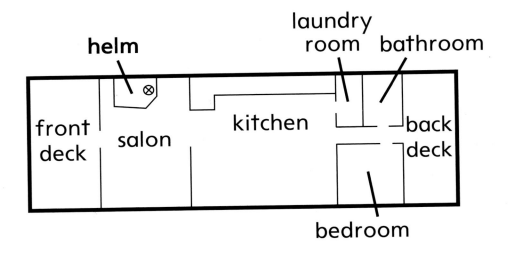

helm
laundry room
bathroom
front deck
salon
kitchen
back deck
bedroom

Small houseboats have two or more rooms.

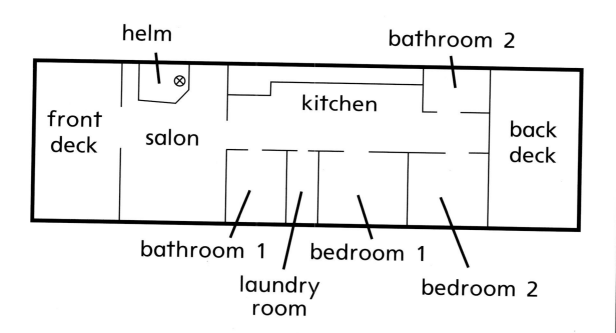

Large houseboats can have seven or more rooms.

Where Do People Talk and Play?

People talk and play in the **salon.**

A salon is like the living room in a house.

The **helm** is in the salon.

The driver steers the houseboat from the helm.

Where Do People Cook and Eat?

People cook food in the kitchen.

The kitchen is sometimes called the galley.

Sometimes the galley is big.

Then, there is room for people
to eat there.

Where Do People Sleep?

People sleep in bedrooms.

Most houseboats have two or more bedrooms.

The beds are part of the houseboat.

The closets and **dressers** are part of the houseboat, too.

Where Do People Take Baths?

People on a houseboat take baths in bathrooms.

Most houseboats have two or more bathrooms.

television

The bathrooms have a toilet, sink, bathtub, and shower.

In this houseboat, you can watch television in the bathtub.

Where Do People Wash Their Clothes?

Some houseboats have a small laundry room.

People can wash their clothes while they are on the boat.

But some people must take their clothes to a **laundry** on land.

Map Quiz

Where is the **helm?**

How many bathrooms are in this houseboat?

Look for the answers on page 24.

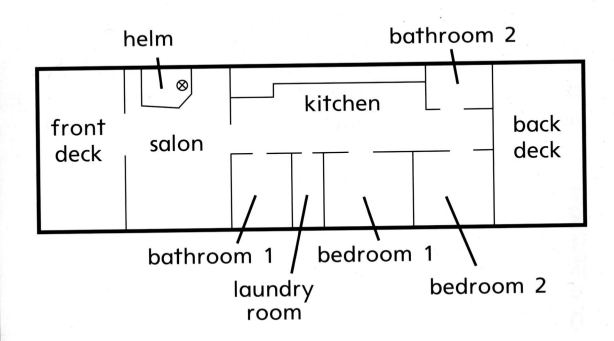

helm

bathroom 2

front deck

salon

kitchen

back deck

bathroom 1

bedroom 1

laundry room

bedroom 2

Picture Glossary

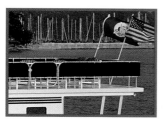

deck
page 7

laundry
page 21

rectangle
page 6

dresser
page 17

motor
pages 4, 5

salon
pages 12, 13

helm
pages 13, 22

23

Note to Parents and Teachers

Reading for information is an important part of a child's literacy development. Learning begins with a question about something. Help children think of themselves as investigators and researchers by encouraging their questions about the world around them. Each chapter in this book begins with a question. Read the question together. Look at the pictures. Talk about what you think the answer might be. Then read the text to find out if your predictions were correct. Think of other questions you could ask about the topic, and discuss where you might find the answers. Use the two simple maps on pages 10 and 11 to introduce children to basic map-reading skills. After discussing the maps, help children draw their own map of a familiar place, such as their room. Assist children in using the picture glossary and the index to practice new vocabulary and research skills.

Index

Answers to quiz on page 22

The **helm** is in the salon.
There are two bathrooms on this houseboat.